Trusting God for Everything
Psalm 23

A PERSONAL RETREAT GUIDE

Trusting God for Everything
Psalm 23

JAN JOHNSON

NAVPRESS

NAVPRESS●.

NavPress is the publishing ministry of The Navigators, an international Christian organization and leader in personal spiritual development. NavPress is committed to helping people grow spiritually and enjoy lives of meaning and hope through personal and group resources that are biblically rooted, culturally relevant, and highly practical.

For a free catalog go to www.NavPress.com
or call 1.800.366.7788 in the United States or 1.800.839.4769 in Canada.

ISBN-13: 978-1-60006-661-0

Cover design by Arvid Wallen
Cover image by Shutterstock

Some of the anecdotal illustrations in this book are true to life and are included with the permission of the persons involved. All other illustrations are composites of real situations, and any resemblance to people living or dead is coincidental.

Printed in the United States of America

1 2 3 4 5 6 7 8 / 13 12 11 10 09

Contents

Introduction: Why Retreat? Making Space for God   7

*Meditation 1: Does God Really Provide Everything
I Need?   17
Psalm 23:1; Ezekiel 34:11-12

*Meditation 2: Trusting God for Soul Restoration   29
Psalm 23:2-3

Meditation 3: Trusting God to Lead   39
Psalm 23:3

*Meditation 4: Trusting God in the Deep Valleys   49
Psalm 23:4

Meditation 5: Trusting That God Is with Me   61
Psalm 23:4

Meditation 6: Trusting God with Those
Who Oppose Me   71
Psalm 23:5

Meditation 7: A Life of Settled Trust in God   83
Psalm 23:6

Notes   95

About the Author   99

If you have time for only three meditations, you might wish to choose
those marked with * (or you might be led to choose otherwise).

Why Retreat?
Making Space
for God

I n an age when daily life and even vacations, tours, and cruises are characterized by pressure-packed schedules, a day of retreat invites us to soul-nurturing rest. Jesus said, "I will give you rest," and he is eager to do that (see Matthew 11:28). A retreat as extended Sabbath renews us as we experience solitude and play at a slower rhythm, allowing God more space to interact with us.

Christians throughout the ages have retreated just as Jesus frequently retreated (see Matthew 4:1-11; 14:13,23; 17:1-9; 26:36-46; Mark 6:31; Luke 5:16; 6:12). The format now used of spending the night away from home was begun by very busy Christian workers (those industrious Jesuits) who needed to pause and reflect on their lives. Sometimes their retreats consisted of a day or two; other times, thirty days or more.

Retreat is an attitude as much as a specific event and place. Once you're practiced at it, even a morning in the park can be a retreat. You learn to set aside worries that you'll be bored or lonely. You let yourself be intrigued by the amazing interaction with God in ways you don't expect; you let yourself be calmed by rest that you've needed for a long time.

What a Retreat Is Not

A retreat is not work. It is a sacred space for rest and reflection. Your goal is not to *cover* Bible passages. Instead, by entering deeply into just a few of them, you'll interact with God about how they speak into your life. Your goal is not to come home and feel that you have *achieved* anything. This retreat is not about what you can *do*. It's about interacting with God gently and knowing more about God's true self. Do you believe that God loves you just for your own self, or do you have to be *doing* something to be loved?

The point of this retreat is to help you build a relationship with God. A relationship involves regular personal interaction, ongoing connection, and shared life experiences. You will experience more deeply (yet also gently) what it means to have a life "in God" or "in Christ," as Paul liked to put it.

A retreat is not a nonstop Bible study. Scripture is used as a vital point of contact with God in order to have real conversations with God in each session. This process is based on what is called *lectio divina*, a way that people have prayerfully read the Bible for centuries. Today people often use self-directed effort to apply the Bible to themselves as if to correct themselves through their own strength. In this retreat, come to the Word to be "taught by the Spirit" (1 Corinthians 2:13), which may or may not be correction but just something we need to know. This sort of dialogue is essential to life in Christ.

In these conversations, the Holy Spirit will mentor you by "ask[ing] you questions you hadn't thought of, challenging you to think in new ways, dropping a few gems to capture your imagination, and allowing you to try on a few ideas before guiding you to the true nature of the issue at hand."[1] Expect to be drawn in by the Holy Spirit so that you may not at times be able to "tell where God's words leave off and your intuitive thoughts begin."[2] Now and then, you'll be tempted to launch off onto a tangent, which is sometimes a good idea but other times a distraction from your conversation with God. If you're the kind of person who usually goes off on tangents, resist for a moment and continue focusing on what's in front of you. See what happens. If you don't usually go off on tangents but you get the urge to now, go with it.

Bring a journal of some kind—a spiral notebook or any booklet will do—on your retreat in case you need to write beyond the space provided. Writing in this guide or in a journal isn't something for you to do or complete; it's a way for you to dialogue with God in a concrete way. Don't *try* to journal; just write what goes through your mind.

Don't expect to come home a different person. You probably will be, but not in the ways you notice at first. In fact, you may notice a shift within yourself only after you've been home a few days. But don't look for it. Let God show you what you need to know.

Don't take a retreat because it sounds like a trendy spiritual thing to do. Do it only because you're drawn to do so. Pay attention to the inner nudge. You may be drawn by weariness. You may be drawn by a longing to be with God. You may be drawn for reasons you don't completely understand. If you're doing a retreat only because someone told you that you should, that may create resentment and detract from your experience.

A so-called successful retreat occurs when we keep our "expectations low and the activities quite simple. When we expect our [retreat] to be highly 'spiritual,' it becomes one more thing to do, continuing the addiction to productivity that is so common in our culture."[3]

How Long?

If you'd like to take a personal retreat but you're not sure how to do it, begin by spending a morning in the park once a week for several weeks. Get used to that until you love it and long for more. You can use this guide, one session per week. When you're ready for an overnight retreat, plan for it to be too short rather than too long (but at least twenty-four hours). Leave wishing you could stay longer. Then you'll be ready to come back.

If you want to use this guide for a one-day retreat, you'll need only three sessions at the most. Choose from the seven sessions listed in the contents section, perhaps the ones with the asterisk (*) by them. Choose the ones that most appeal to you.

If you're taking a longer retreat, complete only two or three sessions a day unless you are refreshed and ready to dig in. You will not interact with God well in the sessions unless you have allowed sufficient space to "be" and are well rested. So don't rush, but don't become bored. In general, meeting with God in the morning, afternoon, and evening will be about right. But if you are tired, skip the afternoon one and take a nap or skip the evening one and sit on the porch instead.

If you have time to complete all seven sessions, feel free to skip some and repeat ones in which you sense God particularly speaking to you. In fact, "repetitions" (repeating a session) are a common retreat practice, and the second experience of a session is often better than the first.

The sessions will not be study sessions but times of conversation with God. Feel free to stop to write or think whenever you need to. Try not to let a session last more than ninety minutes. If you're tired, you may find that as little as thirty to forty-five minutes wears you out. See what works best for you.

If you're drawn to a passage other than the ones provided, pause and ask yourself why. Is anything driving you to this passage other than God's direction? (For example, you have to teach on that passage or write an assignment on it.) If you sense that it is specifically God leading you, go ahead and immerse yourself in it in a meditative way.

As you move through the session, feel free to innovate and do things not suggested in the guide. You'll notice that at times you're asked to read the passage slowly. You're on retreat, so you can afford to move slowly and read slowly. Let the words settle within you. At times, you'll be asked to read the passage aloud. Let the words fall on your ears so that you are hearing them as if for the first time. These are the words of your Beloved to you. Cherish each word. Taste and see that God is good.

Space is provided in this guide for you to write your answers. One reason for this is that you will think more clearly if you write things down instead of just muddling through them in your mind. Another reason is that you can then revisit your retreat after you've been home for a while.

In Between Sessions

Begin your day slowly and move slowly all day. Even if you hike or walk, do that slowly. Eat your breakfast slowly. Live by the clock as little as possible. Breathe deeply and take in every color, sound, and texture around you.

After your first session, listen to what's going on inside you. You might need to:

- Take a nap.
- Do something active, such as taking a walk, hiking, swimming, or doing relaxing exercises.
- Just sit and stare. Try "porch sitting," in which you sit and think about nothing in particular. Find a spot to view birds and trees, if possible, and supply yourself with something to drink and a blank pad of paper. You don't have to write anything, but if you wish to, be ready. Or you may wish to sit in a Jacuzzi.
- Do something creative. You might wish to bring art materials (or even a book of art reproductions to look

at), a musical instrument, binoculars to watch birds, or perhaps materials needed for you to work with your hands (woodworking, needlework, beadwork). Regarding such work with your hands: You must not try to get anything accomplished and you don't want it to be mentally taxing (because your mind must be free to rest and linger on what you might be hearing from God). You are doing the activity for fun.

- Do light, meditative reading. You might bring favorite magazine articles that have helped you in the past or books through which God has spoken to you. Read again the underlined parts. Don't bring a detective novel or something that will engage you wholly.

- Use worship music, but remember to enjoy a lot of silence.

Because you are letting your mind rest, these in-between moments will provide space to "connect the dots" from what you lack to what you need. Ideas will coalesce and you'll be surprised at what comes to you. The downtime will create space for you to hear God.

Develop a rhythm for your day(s) that includes rest, prayer periods, time to sit and stare, play (walking, hiking, working with your hands, looking at an art book; avoid video games). Rest a great deal. Look deeply at everything around you. End your day the same way, such as with a certain prayer or staring at the stars.

Retreating as a Group

Three or four people might want to take their retreat together by staying at the same location (with separate rooms for sleeping and just "being") and meeting a few times a day. This can be as varied as a few people at a retreat center or a bunch of guys on a fishing trip. All should agree on times to be alone and times to meet.

Sessions together might include one or two of these:

- Discussion of what happened during their times alone, how they heard God; this might include reading of what was written in their journals
- Mealtime
- Evenings of being together but being quiet, perhaps each reading or doing artwork or tending a campfire
- Saying a pre-bedtime, evening prayer together

Participants should guard each other's quiet and work hard at not being intrusive, respecting God's ability to speak to each of us.

Preparation for Your Retreat

Start gathering what you'll need, especially hiking gear and things for your creative outlets. You may wish to bring any recording you have of Psalm 23 put to music. Pray about how God might want to nurture you on this retreat. Ask someone who cares about you to pray for you while you're gone, especially if you're often plagued with worry or regret. Count on God's help to let go of those things.

Choosing a Retreat Site

Two important questions to consider are these:

- Do you want to fix your own food and eat by yourself (a secluded place or a retreat center hermitage), or would you rather be at a retreat center where you will eat with others three times a day?

- What sort of physical activity do you want to participate in (hiking, Jacuzzi-sitting, fishing)?

A retreat center is better than a resort getaway because it will promote quiet. It might have:

- A worshipping community of monks or nuns who invite you to join in certain short offices (services) throughout the day
- A fireplace that you might enjoy tending
- A piano you can play if you wish
- A spiritual director (if so, make those arrangements ahead and let the director know the topic you have chosen and how often you'd like to meet)

Can't I Retreat at Home?

Going away takes you away from distractions and gives you a different, more relaxed attitude. If you absolutely cannot get away (even for a morning in the park), remove all distractions (turn off telephones; do not turn on a computer or television; do not answer the door). Take everything that you will need to a place in your house or apartment that does not remind you of work and distractions. Keeping a lit candle in that room might help you quiet yourself and focus.

If you don't have much time when you'll be home alone, you might wish to do just one session a week. If so, try to go through the session the same day of the week and at the same time. This will develop a retreat rhythm in your life.

Reentry into Home, Family, and Community

Before leaving your retreat site, pause. Thank God for this extended time. As you near home, start picturing the people who might be there, what they need from you, and what your tasks will be. Thank God for these people and ask God to help you welcome them. Once you arrive, keep moving as slowly as possible.

As the days pass, continue to journal about the ideas you absorbed during the retreat. Reread your journal.

Make notes on what worked well about your personal retreat (location, setting, timing) so that your next retreat will bring an even more natural tendency to rest in God.

Does God Really Provide Everything I Need?

The psalms give us a picture of what it looks like when we live in the kingdom of God here and now every day. That overflowing life exists not only in the future, but also now: "The kingdom of God is within you" (Luke 17:21). Such a life of connecting with God moves us toward becoming people who live with joy and gratefulness, being able to bless enemies (difficult people), going the extra mile, living with purposeful intentionality, letting go of pride, and never judging.[1] This is the life humans were meant to live. In one of Jesus' many "shepherd moments," he said, "Do not be afraid, little flock, for your Father has been pleased to give you the kingdom" (Luke 12:32). This life in the kingdom of God is a life of confidence in God.

Opening to God's Message

Find a comfortable, pleasant spot to settle that will not present distractions.

Why are you taking this retreat? What do you most need from God in your life right now? What do you most need to understand from God right now?

At what moments in life are you convinced you don't have everything that you need? Give a few lighthearted answers (when I see a new car or purse or vacation out of my price range) and a few serious answers (job has ended; precisely needed medication not affordable). Answer as honestly as you can.

Immersed in God's Message

BACKGROUND: *Confidence psalms* While many psalms are thanksgiving psalms composed after being delivered from a crisis, confidence psalms "are more distanced from the crisis and reflective. They speak generically of a relationship with Yahweh that is utterly trustworthy in the face of *every* threat. . . . The speaker of these poems cannot imagine a situation that would cause doubt or trouble enough to jeopardize the trust. The relationship has been tested severely, and Yahweh has shown himself to be profoundly reliable and powerful. That is to be celebrated."[2] In confidence psalms, psalmists take what God says and make it their own from the depths of themselves. This guide focuses solely on Psalm 23 because it is a confidence psalm.

To quiet yourself and focus before reading the Scripture passage, say this slowly:

In our meditation we ponder the chosen text on the strength of the promise that it has something utterly personal to say to us today and for our Christian life.[3]

Read this passage aloud very slowly. Because it's probably familiar, you might be tempted to rush through it.

The LORD is my shepherd; I shall not want.

He maketh me to lie down in green pastures: he leadeth me beside the still waters.

He restoreth my soul: he leadeth me in the paths of righteousness for his name's sake.

Yea, though I walk through the valley of the shadow of death, I will fear no evil: for thou art with me; thy rod and thy staff they comfort me. . . .

For this is what the Sovereign LORD says: "I myself will search for my sheep and look after them. As a shepherd looks after his scattered flock when he is with them, so will I look after my sheep. I will rescue them from all the places where they were scattered on a day of clouds and darkness." . . .

The Lord is my shepherd; I have everything I need. (Psalm 23:1-4, KJV; Ezekiel 34:11-12, NIV; Psalm 23:1, GNT)

Before reading the passage again, consider:

CONTEXT: God as shepherd is a familiar image in Scripture (see Psalm 79:13; 80:1; Isaiah 40:11; Jeremiah 23:3-4). The shepherd image is also used by and applied to Jesus, which is why it is appropriate to transfer the meaning of Psalm 23 to Jesus as well (see John 10:11,14,27-30; Hebrews 13:20; 1 Peter 2:25; 5:4; Revelation 7:17).

BACKGROUND: Picture the work of a shepherd as you read this psalm.

- **Protector of sheep:** The shepherd defends the sheep from wild dogs, cougars, and rustlers. A shepherd also protects the sheep from the environment by providing shelter from storms and blizzards.

- **Provider of food and clean water (instead of stagnant, muddy water):** The shepherd manages the food supply by leading sheep where they will find adequate pasture instead of leaving them in bare brown fields.

- **Doctor:** The shepherd tends the wounds and diseases of the sheep and has to keep constantly alert to spot their injuries.

- **Disciplinarian:** The shepherd monitors fights among the sheep and protects smaller or wounded ones.

- **Rescuer:** When sheep get lost or wander into dangerous places, the shepherd must search relentlessly. That might involve climbing down into crevices or coming close to poisonous snakes in order to rescue the sheep.

- **Companion:** The shepherd walks with and among the sheep and knows them by name. The sheep of different shepherds can be kept in the same pen because when a shepherd comes to the pen and calls for his or her sheep, only that shepherd's sheep will come.

- **Delighted manager:** Speaking of God as a shepherd, Phillip Keller wrote, "For Him there is no greater reward, no deeper satisfaction, than that of seeing His sheep contented, well fed, safe and flourishing under His care. This is indeed His very 'life.' He lays Himself out for those who are His."[4]

A shepherd who is gentle, kind, intelligent, brave, and selfless (as God is) is much preferred to a careless, selfish one who would cause the sheep to struggle, starve, and suffer hardship.

MEANINGS OF WORDS: *I shall not want* is also well translated "I have everything I need." Try saying that last phrase aloud slowly. How many people do you know who would say that and mean it? This is a radical statement in a culture flooded with advertising—an industry whose primary goal is to convince you that you *don't* have everything you need. The Israelites would have felt lack many times, yet "Israel refuses to split things into spiritual and material. It affirms that Yahweh is the satisfaction of all wants and needs . . . of every kind of need."[5]

Here are some other paraphrases:

- I am completely satisfied with God's management of my life.
- I can't think of anything God could give me that would make me more content.
- I don't need a thing.

The statement "I have everything I need" brings up issues that will not be resolved in this session:

- Do I believe God has done well by me? (Meditations 4–6 especially)
- What do I believe about the times in my life that have been difficult?
- Have I perhaps struck an unspoken bargain with God that I'll believe and follow but I expect my life not to include difficult times?

Most people find these questions challenging. This psalm presents a radical picture of what it looks like to trust God. If you don't feel authentic saying, "The Lord is my shepherd and I have everything I need," feel free to add *maybe* or *sometimes* at the beginning or end.

That's a realistic way to aim toward an attitude of complete trust.

As you read the passage, consider what word or phrase stands out to you or resonates with you.

- Waiting for a word to stand out is not a spooky or magical thing. This is a natural thing that probably already happens to you when you read the Bible—you think: *How come I never saw that word or phrase or idea before?* Actually, you did see it before, but now you see it in a new and different way. It now stands out to you.
- Don't feel pressured to make something up. If nothing stands out, quiet yourself, read the quieting exercise ("In our meditation we ponder the chosen text . . ." and read the passage again.
- Don't use self-directed effort to try to apply the passage to yourself. When you attempt to apply a passage, you try to figure out what you should do to implement what you read. At this point, simply let God bring to you what you need to know. Let it be God's effort, not your own.
- Be open to letting God speak to you. Expect to be surprised.

Now reread the passage again slowly aloud.

The LORD is my shepherd; I shall not want.
He maketh me to lie down in green pastures: he leadeth me
     beside the still waters.
He restoreth my soul: he leadeth me in the paths of
     righteousness for his name's sake.
Yea, though I walk through the valley of the shadow of death,
     I will fear no evil: for thou art with me; thy rod and thy
     staff they comfort me. . . .

For this is what the Sovereign Lord says: "I myself will search for my sheep and look after them. As a shepherd looks after his scattered flock when he is with them, so will I look after my sheep. I will rescue them from all the places where they were scattered on a day of clouds and darkness." . . .

The Lord is my shepherd; I have everything I need.

Write down the word, phrase, or idea that stands out to you.

What feelings did you get in these verses?

What thoughts or impressions come to you? What connections do you make? What questions or perhaps objections do you have? Does anything surprise you?

What might God be saying to you through what has stood out in this passage?

Responding to God's Message

Read the passage again to yourself and consider how it leads you to dialogue with God.

> The LORD is my shepherd; I shall not want.
> He maketh me to lie down in green pastures: he leadeth me
>   beside the still waters.
> He restoreth my soul: he leadeth me in the paths of
>   righteousness for his name's sake.
> Yea, though I walk through the valley of the shadow of death,
>   I will fear no evil: for thou art with me; thy rod and thy
>   staff they comfort me. . . .

> For this is what the Sovereign LORD says: "I myself will search for my sheep and look after them. As a shepherd looks after his scattered flock when he is with them, so will I look after my sheep. I will rescue them from all the places where they were scattered on a day of clouds and darkness." . . .

> The Lord is my shepherd; I have everything I need.

Say to God what you most need to say. It will help if you write your prayer in the space provided or say it aloud. Doing so will make it more concrete and relational. Be open to having a dialogue with God, to being gently led by the Holy Spirit.

If you write your prayer, you might want to begin with "Dear God" or "Dear Jesus" and then say what you need to say in response to what Jesus has said in the passage to you. If you're not sure what to write, here are some possibilities:

- Begin with, "I'm so glad that you said . . ." or "I really needed to hear that you . . ."
- Feel free to say things that don't sound spiritual (such as, "What if I don't really believe that . . . ?"). Then move on with more you need to say.
- Tell God what you don't understand.
- Ask questions. Put a star by these because you may find them answered by the end of today or tomorrow.
- Never feel pressed to write pages and pages. One sentence might really be enough, or you might need to write more.

Resting with God in the Message

Read the passage (or the portion that stood out to you) again to yourself one more time.

The LORD is my shepherd; I shall not want.
He maketh me to lie down in green pastures: he leadeth me
  beside the still waters.
He restoreth my soul: he leadeth me in the paths of
  righteousness for his name's sake.

Yea, though I walk through the valley of the shadow of death, I will fear no evil: for thou art with me; thy rod and thy staff they comfort me. . . .

For this is what the Sovereign LORD says: "I myself will search for my sheep and look after them. As a shepherd looks after his scattered flock when he is with them, so will I look after my sheep. I will rescue them from all the places where they were scattered on a day of clouds and darkness." . . .

The Lord is my shepherd; I have everything I need.

As you've read the passage several times, how have you experienced God? What was God like? Reflect on how God seemed to you. Did you have a sense that you're only talking to yourself or that God was present? Did God seem distant or attentive? Caring or frustrated? Demanding or inviting? Talk to God about this.

Allow yourself time to soak in what has come to you — questions, new ideas, and clarifications about God or yourself. Let it sink all the way down to where you really live. Sit for a few moments and ponder what has transpired. You might wish to:

- Sit and just "be" with God.
- Appreciate or celebrate what occurred in your conversation with God.
- Worship God in some way (even dancing, singing a favorite song, or drawing).
- Rest in the idea that you are the dwelling place of God and that God wants to build a home in you.

Close the interaction with this prayer:

May today there be peace within.
May I trust you, God, that you can work in me exactly
    where I am.
May I not forget the infinite possibilities born of faith.
May I use those gifts I have received and pass on the love
    that has been given to me.
May I be content knowing I am your child.
Let your presence settle into my bones and allow my soul
    the freedom to sing, dance, praise, and love.
        —THÉRÈSE OF LISIEUX (PARAPHRASED)

Move into a time of enjoying the life and breath God gave you.
You might want to:

- Take a nap
- Take a walk, hike, swim, or do relaxing exercises
- Try "porch sitting," watching birds and trees, or sitting in a
  Jacuzzi
- Do a creative activity (using art materials, woodworking,
  needlework, beadwork), without trying to accomplish
  anything
- Do light, meditative reading (not a detective novel or
  something that engages you wholly)

Trusting God for Soul Restoration

After the psalmist makes the radical statement that he lacks nothing because the Lord really is his shepherd and he really does have everything he needs, he paints some odd pictures of what this looks like. The pictures are odd because they aren't like many other psalms, which often picture the psalmist as thirsty for God and longing for God:

> As the deer pants for streams of water,
>   so my soul pants for you, O God.
> My soul thirsts for God, for the living God.
>   When can I go and meet with God?
> My tears have been my food
>   day and night,
> while men say to me all day long,
>   "Where is your God?" (Psalm 42:1-3)

Although the psalmist in Psalm 42 is experiencing God's absence, even feeding on tears, Psalm 23 presents a radical picture of confidence and reassurance. In Psalm 23, the psalmist says that the shepherd is right there providing everything he needs. Psalm 42 is about a soul that is thirsty and starving for God, but Psalm 23 presents a picture of a soul that is nurtured, protected, and deeply satisfied with God's companionship.

Sometimes we live in Psalm 42—starving and thirsty—but we can gradually move toward the restored and satisfied condition described in Psalm 23.

Opening to God's Message

Settle in the same space as the last meditation unless that proved to be distracting. (If the previous session is still resonating with you, pause for a moment. Do you want to do it again? If so, this is what retreatants call "repetitions." You may need to go deeper or broader.)

When was the last time you felt perfectly relaxed?

Was that feeling attached to a location, an activity, or a person? If so, why?

Immersed in God's Message

To quiet yourself and focus before reading the Scripture passage, say this slowly:

> *In our meditation we ponder the chosen text on the strength of the promise that it has something utterly personal to say to us today and for our Christian life.*[1]

Read this passage aloud very slowly.

The LORD is my shepherd, I shall not want.
    He makes me lie down in green pastures;
he leads me beside still waters;
    he restores my soul.
He leads me in right paths
    for his name's sake.

Even though I walk through the darkest valley,
    I fear no evil;
for you are with me;
    your rod and your staff—
    they comfort me.

You prepare a table before me
    in the presence of my enemies;
you anoint my head with oil;
    my cup overflows.
Surely goodness and mercy shall follow me
    all the days of my life,
and I shall dwell in the house of the LORD

my whole life long. . . .
[Pause]
   He makes me lie down in green pastures;
he leads me beside still waters;
   he restores my soul. (Psalm 23:1-6,2-3, NRSV)

Before reading the passage again, consider:

PICTURING THE PASSAGE: *Green* pastures conjures up fresh and tender grass that is comfortable to lie down in, inviting rest and enjoyment.

PICTURING THE PASSAGE: *Still waters* can be translated "waters of rest,"[2] especially at noon in the heat of the day in the Middle East. Skilled shepherds not only know where the good watering places are but also might have worked hard to make a small dam in the stream or wadi and maneuver water in accessible places. If not led to still, quiet, deep, clean, pure water, sheep may drink from polluted potholes full of parasites.[3]

PICTURING THE PASSAGE: Why *lie down*? Once sheep have found green pasture, they're likely to stand there and eat, but the sheep in the psalm does not. (Imagine yourself in your favorite restaurant simply looking around but not ordering anything.) Why would sheep lie down instead of eat? Only if they are full and satisfied, only if they have everything they need, only if the Lord is their shepherd.

But sheep will not lie down unless they are free of all fear: free from friction with other sheep; free from hunger; free from flies and parasites; free from any tension and aggravation. Shepherds must provide sheep release from these obstacles; the sheep cannot help themselves.[4] Untended, hungry, ill-fed sheep do not lie down; they are always on the move. Close your eyes and picture a sheep lying down in green pastures, perfectly contented, safe, and satisfied.

PICTURING THE PASSAGE: Why does the shepherd lead the sheep *beside* still waters instead of to the still waters to drink? Because the sheep are not thirsty (like the deer in Psalm 42) but perfectly content. The sheep are refreshed and restored and content to be led wherever the shepherd goes.

MEANING OF WORDS: *Restore* means to "bring back vitality,"[5] to "bring back the soul that is as it were flown away, so that it comes to itself again, therefore to impart new life, *recreare*. This [God] does to the soul, by causing it amidst the drying and heat of temptation and trouble, to taste the very essence of life which refreshes and strengthens it."[6] Please read that again. It is a description of how God meets us in retreat and what God does.

As you prepare to read only verses 1-3, consider what word or phrase resonates with you or stays with you or seems to shimmer for you. Was there a scene or a picture that drew you?

- Don't use self-effort to try to apply the passage to yourself. Simply let God bring to you what you need to know. Let it be God's effort, not your own.
- Be open to letting God speak to you. Expect to be surprised.

Read verses 1-3 aloud slowly.

The LORD is my shepherd, I shall not want.
    He makes me lie down in green pastures;
he leads me beside still waters;
    he restores my soul.

Write down the word, phrase, idea, or picture that stands out to you.

What feelings did you get from what stood out to you?

What thoughts or impressions come to you? What connections do you make? What questions or perhaps objections do you have? Does anything surprise you?

What might God be saying to you through what has stood out in this passage? Is there a place in your life where you really need to know what comes to you from the passage? Take a few minutes to do this. If your mind begins to drift, come back to the word or phrase that stood out to you.

Responding to God's Message

Read verses 1-3 again and consider how you're led to dialogue with God.

The LORD is my shepherd, I shall not want.
    He makes me lie down in green pastures;
he leads me beside still waters;
    he restores my soul.

Write down or say aloud what you need to say back to God because of what God has said to you in these verses. (Writing or saying it aloud will help you get out of your head and respond to God concretely.) Be open to having a dialogue with God, to being gently led by the Holy Spirit.

If you're not sure what to pray, begin with the word or image that drew you. Tell God:

- Why the phrase or picture drew you
- Where and why you have not sensed that soul restoration, green pastures, or still waters
- Where you have sensed that soul restoration, green pastures, or still waters
- How much you do or don't want this life of satisfaction with God, of lying down in green pastures

"TRYING ON" THE PSALM: Read the following paraphrase in a confident tone of voice. Don't worry if you don't mean every word it says or even most words. For now you're trying on the idea of living your life in the kingdom of God—of trusting God, no matter what. This is not dishonest; you're "putting on" the new self in Christ (see Colossians 3:10).

You really are my shepherd. You really do give me everything
I need.
You really do make me lie down in green pastures and lead me
beside still waters.
You really do restore my soul.

If you weren't able to read the paraphrase confidently, try it again. Don't monitor how true or untrue it is—just try it on.

Tell God how it felt to try it on this way.

Resting with God in the Message

Read verses 1-3 again to yourself one more time (or read them as previously paraphrased, "You really are my shepherd," and so on).

> The LORD is my shepherd, I shall not want.
>> He makes me lie down in green pastures;
> he leads me beside still waters;
>> he restores my soul.

As you've read the passage several times, how have you experienced God? What was God like? Reflect on how God seemed to you. Did God seem distant or attentive? Tell God about it.

Allow yourself time to soak in what has come to you — questions, new ideas, and clarifications about God or yourself. Let it sink all the way down to where you really live. Sit for a few moments and ponder what has transpired. You may wish to:

- Sit and just "be" with God.
- Appreciate or celebrate what occurred in your conversation with God.
- Worship God by singing a song related to Psalm 23 (or even dancing to it). If you brought a recording of a Psalm 23 song, play it now. Close your eyes and listen.
- Worship God by drawing the scene in verse 2: the kind of pasture that would be ideal for a sheep to lie down in.
- Go and lie down in the grass. Lie there and imagine the contentment of being fully satisfied.
- Rest in the idea that God delights in you and in taking care of you.

Close the interaction with this prayer:

May today there be peace within.
May I trust you, God, that you can work in me exactly
    where I am.
May I not forget the infinite possibilities born of faith.
May I use those gifts I have received and pass on the love
    that has been given to me.
May I be content knowing I am your child.
Let your presence settle into my bones and allow my soul
    the freedom to sing, dance, praise, and love.
    —THÉRÈSE OF LISIEUX (PARAPHRASED)

Move into a time of enjoying the life and breath God gave you.
You might want to:

- Take a nap
- Take a walk, hike, swim, or do relaxing exercises
- Try "porch sitting," watching birds and trees, or sitting in a
  Jacuzzi
- Do a creative activity (using art materials, woodworking,
  needlework, beadwork), without trying to accomplish
  anything
- Do light, meditative reading (not a detective novel or
  something that engages you wholly)

Trusting God to Lead

I t's easier to let God lead us when we live in a state of satisfaction and assurance as pictured by sheep who lie down in green pastures and are being led by still waters. Then we're content to let God lead us minute by minute for the next ten minutes or next sixty minutes instead of living in a state of *But what if . . . ?* We trust God and know that God will direct us not by preaching at us but by simply guiding us step-by-step. As we learn to follow intently behind the Shepherd, we discover a deep inner goodness about God that is very attractive and makes us want to follow carefully.

Opening to God's Message

Settle in the same space as before unless that proved to be distracting. (If the previous session is still resonating with you, pause for a moment. Do you want to do it again? If so, this is what retreatants call "repetitions." You may need to go deeper or broader.)

What are your questions about God's leading or God's guidance?

What about God's guidance has confused you in the past?

What sort of leading or guidance do you need in the future (especially in relation to the care of your soul)?

Immersed in God's Message

To quiet yourself and focus before reading the Scripture passage, say this slowly:

> *In our meditation we ponder the chosen text on the strength of the promise that it has something utterly personal to say to us today and for our Christian life.*[1]

Read this passage aloud very slowly.

He leadeth me in the paths of righteousness for his name's sake. . . .

GOD, my shepherd!
    I don't need a thing.
You have bedded me down in lush meadows,
    you find me quiet pools to drink from.

True to your word,
> you let me catch my breath
> and send me in the right direction. . . .
> He renews my strength.
He guides me along right paths,
> bringing honor to his name. . . .
He leadeth me in the paths of righteousness for his name's
sake. (Psalm 23:3, KJV; 23:1-3, MSG; 23:3, NLT; 23:3, KJV)

Before reading the verses again, consider:

MEANING OF WORDS: *leads, guides* An Eastern shepherd gently guides sheep by walking ahead of the flock[2] so they can follow. Speaking of himself as the Good Shepherd, Jesus said, "When [the shepherd] has brought out all his own [sheep], he *goes on ahead of them*, and his sheep *follow him* because they know his voice. . . . My sheep listen to my voice; I know them, and they follow me" (John 10:4,27, emphasis added). Just as sheep had so many trails they could get lost on, we may not be sure what to do or where to go, but we follow along behind the shepherd.

MEANING OF WORDS AND PHRASES: *Paths of righteousness* is frequently translated "right paths," meaning paths that lead to deliverance from trouble and enemies and into God's joy.

Nowadays the idea of *righteousness* (as well as the word) has become stuffy. People don't aspire to it because they perceive it to be about being goody-goody people who think they know everything and always appear good and are sometimes eager to tell you where you're wrong.

The true idea of *righteousness* in Scripture is about "what that is about a person that makes him or her really right or good" or "true inner goodness. . . . It represents a combination of skill, wisdom, power, and steadfastness for good that makes it very attractive."[3] So righteous paths are not boring or oppressive activities you'd never want to take anyway but the *deepest sort of attractive way of being* that you've always wanted. Maybe you know someone like this—deeply good but also delightfully pleasant. Such a good and true and beautiful person reflects life in the kingdom of God.

He leads me in paths of righteousness This leadership by God is not only showing us which path but also enabling us to walk that path. Many *paths of righteousness* seem too advanced for our capabilities. And frankly they are. But as we trust in God as our shepherd and trust that we really do have everything we need, we are surprisingly enabled to walk paths that surpass our natural tendencies. Afterward, we marvel that *we* ever did it!

MEANING OF WORDS: *for his name's sake* In Scripture, *name* is equivalent to character or reputation. These verses mean that God provides green pastures and still waters "because He has a reputation among His saints for faithful dealings with them."[4] "True to your word" is an accurate paraphrase (MSG) because "for his name's sake" (KJV) is like saying, "And what else would you expect God to do—since God is so full of steadfast love and mercy?"

The *name* also referred to a person's presence and power: "God leads me in paths that radiate God's divine presence and power."

GOD'S SHEPHERD-STYLE LEADERSHIP: When people want guidance from God, they generally want God to give them the destination and then they'll manage to get there. But God is not like that. God is like a shepherd. The shepherd does not tell the sheep the destination. But that's okay with the sheep because they understand that their shepherd's leadership is one step at a time and they're very content to follow without demanding more information. Why? Because they trust the shepherd. The more we trust that the Lord is our shepherd and we really do have everything we need, the more we are content with knowing only the next step.

As you read the Scripture passage aloud again, consider what word, phrase, image, or idea resonates with you. Be open to letting

God speak to you. Expect to be surprised.

> He leadeth me in the paths of righteousness for his name's
> sake. . . .

> GOD, my shepherd!
>   I don't need a thing.
> You have bedded me down in lush meadows,
>   you find me quiet pools to drink from.
> True to your word,
>   you let me catch my breath
>   and send me in the right direction. . . .
>   He renews my strength.
> He guides me along right paths,
>   bringing honor to his name. . . .
> He leadeth me in the paths of righteousness for his name's
>   sake.

Write down the word, phrase, or idea that stands out to you.

What feelings do you get in these verses?

What thoughts or impressions come to you? What connections do you make? What questions or perhaps objections do you have? Does anything surprise you?

What might God be saying to you through what has stood out in this passage? Is there a place in your life where you need to trust God's guidance or deep goodness or desire and reliability to give you everything you need? Or where you long for these things? Take a few minutes to do this. If your mind begins to drift, come back to the word or phrase that stood out to you.

Responding to God's Message

Read the passage again slowly to yourself and consider how it leads you to dialogue with God.

> He leadeth me in the paths of righteousness for his name's sake. . . .

> GOD, my shepherd!
>   I don't need a thing.
> You have bedded me down in lush meadows,
>   you find me quiet pools to drink from.
> True to your word,
>   you let me catch my breath
>   and send me in the right direction. . . .

He renews my strength.
He guides me along right paths,
     bringing honor to his name. . . .
He leadeth me in the paths of righteousness for his name's
     sake.

Write in the space provided or say aloud what you need to say back to God. Be open to having a dialogue with God, to being gently led by the Holy Spirit. If you're not sure how to start, here are some possibilities:

- Talk with God about this idea of following step-by-step without knowing the destination. How do you feel about that?
- Ask God for help in following divine guidance.
- Ask questions and put a star by them because you might find them answered by the end of today or tomorrow.
- Ask God to show you what deep inner goodness looks like.
- Begin with, "I'm so glad that you said . . ." or "I really needed to hear that you . . ."
- Never feel pressed to write pages and pages. One sentence might really be enough, or you may need to write more.

"TRYING ON" THE PSALM: Read the following paraphrase aloud in a confident tone of voice. Don't worry if you don't mean every word it says. For now, just try putting on this new self that trusts God for everything (see Colossians 3:10).

> GOD, you really are my shepherd! I don't need a thing.
> You have bedded me down in lush meadows, you find me quiet pools to drink from.
> True to your word, you let me catch my breath and send me in the right direction. Thank you!

If you weren't able to read the paraphrase confidently, try it again.

Tell God how it felt to try it on this way.

Resting with God in the Message

Read the passage again to yourself one more time (or read it as paraphrased, "You really are my shepherd," and so on).

As you've read the passage several times, how have you experienced God? What was God like? Close your eyes and reflect on how God seemed to you. Talk to God about this.

Allow yourself time to soak in what has come to you — questions, new ideas, and clarifications about God or yourself. Let it sink all the way down to where you really live. Sit for a few moments and ponder what has transpired. You might wish to:

- Sit and just "be" with God.
- Appreciate or celebrate what occurred in your conversation with God.
- Worship God by singing a song related to Psalm 23 (or even dancing to it). If you brought a recording of a Psalm 23 song, play it now. Close your eyes and listen.
- Walk along a path. Imagine what it's like not worrying about where you're going but just following behind Jesus.
- Rest in the idea that God delights in you and in taking care of you.

Close the interaction with this prayer:

May today there be peace within.
May I trust you, God, that you can work in me exactly
    where I am.
May I not forget the infinite possibilities born of faith.
May I use those gifts I have received and pass on the love
    that has been given to me.
May I be content knowing I am your child.
Let your presence settle into my bones and allow my soul
    the freedom to sing, dance, praise, and love.
      —THÉRÈSE OF LISIEUX (PARAPHRASED)

Move into a time of enjoying the life and breath God gave you.
You might want to:

- Take a nap
- Take a walk, hike, swim, or do relaxing exercises
- Try "porch sitting," watching birds and trees, or sitting in a Jacuzzi
- Do a creative activity (using art materials, woodworking,

needlework, beadwork), without trying to accomplish anything

- Do light, meditative reading (not a detective novel or something that engages you wholly)

Trusting God in the Deep Valleys

F ear is what keeps us from believing that the Lord is really our shepherd and from trusting that we have everything we need today. That's one reason that one of the most frequent commands of Scripture is "Do not be afraid." This instruction is given again and again—by God, by angels, by Jesus, by prophets and apostles.[1] God said it to Abraham, Moses, and Joshua. An angel said it to Mary and Zechariah. Jesus said it to several people but especially to the disciples, telling them not to be afraid of the power they saw in a miraculous catch of fish, of the earth's terrifying elements, or of men who would beat and persecute them (see Luke 5:10; Matthew 8:26; 10:26).

Trust is the opposite of fear. To picture yourself as more trusting, you might ask yourself, *What would I do if I weren't afraid? Afraid of death? Afraid of failing? Afraid of being alone?* This passage tells why we don't have to be afraid and how we can face fear.

Opening to God's Message

Settle in the same space as before unless that proved to be distracting. (If the previous session is still resonating with you, pause for a moment. Do you want to do it again? If so, this is what retreatants call "repetitions." You may need to go deeper or broader.)

Consider the effects fear has on you. Check the following descriptions that apply:

- Fear often causes me to sin. I don't tell the truth for fear it will hurt me or someone else. I don't move forward to help others because I'm afraid of what might happen. I become self-absorbed in holding tightly to what I need because I'm afraid that tomorrow I won't have everything I need.
- Fear is often at the root of anger. I use anger to protect myself against the person or situation I am afraid of.
- Fear often accompanies confusion. In fear, I don't think things through but instead worry that I can't accomplish a certain thing or am not clever enough to do it. (This leads to that little saying "Stress makes you stupid.")

How might your life be different if you weren't afraid?

Immersed in God's Message

SETTING: A day in the life of a sheep means that at noontime it's essential to have a cool place to lie down and still waters to drink from (see Psalm 23:2). But as night approaches, the valley looks darker than usual (see verse 4).

TONE: One of the primary ways to determine the tone of a psalm is to consider who is speaking to whom. Now and then, he shifts from speaking *about* God to speaking *to* God, almost as if the psalmist has turned from pondering about God to raising his hands and praying to God. That shift occurs in this psalm. Instead of speaking of *the Lord* or *he*, as in verses 1-3, the psalmist now shifts to second person: *you, thou.* "The middle section is more immediate and more intense to the faith experience of the speaker. It seems closer to the actual memories of [the psalmist's] deliverance" in the past.[2] This important shift from speaking *about* God to speaking *to* God is what needs to occur in our daily thoughts and in our journal writing. Then all of life (including worry) becomes prayer, addressed to the One we love.

To quiet yourself and focus before reading the passage, say this slowly:

> *In our meditation we ponder the chosen text on the strength of the promise that it has something utterly personal to say to us today and for our Christian life.*[3]

Read this Scripture passage aloud very slowly.

The Lord is my shepherd;
  I have everything I need.
He lets me rest in green meadows;
  he leads me beside peaceful streams.
  He renews my strength.
He guides me along right paths,
  bringing honor to his name.

Even when I walk
  through the dark valley of death,
I will not be afraid,

for you are close beside me.
Your rod and your staff
    protect and comfort me. . . .

Yea, though I walk through the valley of the shadow of
death, I will fear no evil: for thou art with me. (Psalm 23:1-4,
NLT; 4, KJV)

Before reading the passage again, consider:

MEANING OF PHRASES: The *valley of the shadow of death* is
sometimes translated *dark valley of death*. It literally translates as *valley
of deepest darkness* because "the Hebrew word used contains no refer-
ence to death as such but does refer to all dark and bitter experiences."[4]
This would include surprises and all kinds of disasters, anything that
threatens us, creating dread and fear. Such valleys are also filled with
physical or emotional pain, diseases, depression, grief, rejection, fail-
ure, abuse, or endless toil.

Through appears in all translations. No matter what the dangers,
the psalmists gets *through* them to the other side. (When you read the
passage aloud, you may wish to emphasize *through*.)

MEANING OF PHRASE: *Thou art with me* (KJV) is also translated *you are with me* or *you are close beside me* (NIV, NLT). The rod and
staff (mentioned later) are comforting, but the presence of the shepherd himself — *thou* — is the great comfort. This is important because
people of faith sometimes believe they should not go through trials
and they become resentful when they do. *Where is God now?* they
ask. We aren't promised that there will be no trials, but that as we go
through them, God is always our constant companion. God walks
alongside us, and that presence keeps us from being afraid. "It is God's
companionship that transforms every situation. It does not mean there
are no deathly valleys, no enemies. But they are not capable of hurt,
and so the powerful loyalty and solidarity of Yahweh *comfort*, precisely

in situations of threat. . . . Psalm 23 knows that evil is present in the world, but it is not feared."[5]

TURNABOUT OF PHRASE: *I will fear no evil: for thou art with me* is also translated, "I will not be afraid, for you are close beside me" (NLT). In the confidence psalms, psalmists take statements made by God and turn them around and say them from their own perspectives. They make them their own from the depths of themselves. This phrase is an example of that. God often says from the divine perspective, "Fear not, for I am with thee" (Genesis 26:24, KJV). This psalm then takes this frequent wording of God and turns it into a statement of confidence by the hearer: "Fear not" becomes "I will fear no evil," and "I am with thee" becomes "for thou art with me." The psalmist is praying back God's own words to God. This is an excellent thing for us to do in our prayers. This statement of confidence "I will fear no evil: for thou art with me" is a way of saying that the worst will not be as bad as we had thought. I don't have to think, *What if . . . ?* or *Oh no!*

PICTURING THE PASSAGE: You might envision yourself moving through a place of darkness in your past, present, or future or even a place of physical darkness. If it is dark outside, you might want to take your flashlight and finish this meditation outside.

ENTERING INTO THE PASSAGE: What comes to mind when you think of God being with you? Standing behind you to hold on to you? Standing in front of you to shield you? Standing beside you and picking you up as you fall? Write your favorite image here.

As you read the Scripture passage, consider what word, phrase, or picture stands out to you or comes to you (especially from verse 4). Be open to letting God speak to you. Expect to be surprised.

- Don't feel pressured to make something up. If nothing comes to you, quiet yourself, read the quieting exercise ("In our meditation we ponder the chosen text . . ." and read the passage again.

- Don't use self-directed effort to try to apply the passage to yourself. When you attempt to apply a passage, you try to figure out what you should do to implement what you read. At this point, simply let God bring to you what you need to know. Let it be God's effort, not your own.

The LORD is my shepherd;
    I have everything I need.
He lets me rest in green meadows;
    he leads me beside peaceful streams.
    He renews my strength.
He guides me along right paths,
    bringing honor to his name.

Even when I walk
    through the dark valley of death,
I will not be afraid,
    for you are close beside me.
Your rod and your staff
    protect and comfort me. . . .

Write down the word, phrase, or picture that stands out to you in verse 4.

What feelings come to you in these verses? (You may want to jot some notes here.) Take a few minutes to do this.

What thoughts or impressions come to you? What connections do you make? What questions or perhaps objections do you have? Does anything surprise you?

What might God be saying to you through what has stood out in this passage?

Responding to God's Message

Read the Scripture passage again to yourself and consider how it leads you to dialogue with God. Then follow these prompts and write what comes to you.

Yea, though I walk through the valley of the shadow of death,

(Write about how this is or has been true for you.)

I will fear no evil:
(Write about how this has been true for you or you would like for it to be true.)

for thou art with me.
(Write about how this has been true for you or you would like for it to be true.)

Continue to write your response to God because of what came to you in this passage. Be open to having a dialogue with God, to being gently led by the Holy Spirit.

- How much do you want this life of freedom from fear and assurance of God's constant companionship?
- Talk with God about this idea of walking *through* the valley. If God is with you, will you be okay? (Be honest.)
- Ask God for help in getting through.
- Feel free to say things that don't sound spiritual (such as, "I didn't ask for this valley!"). Then move on with more you need to say.

- Begin with, "I'm so glad that you said . . ." or "I really needed to hear that you . . ."

After you're finished praying, try this experiment again.

"TRYING ON" THE PSALM: Read verses 1-4 of the psalm aloud in a confident tone of voice. Don't worry if you don't mean every word it says or even most words. For now you're trying on the idea of living your life in the kingdom of God—of trusting God, no matter what. Even if it doesn't fit, try it on.

You really are my shepherd
You really do give me everything I need.
You really do make me lie in green pastures
  and lead me beside still waters.
You really do restore my soul.
You really do guide me in the best kinds of paths because
  you always do what's best for me.
You really are with me even when I walk through very
  dark things
Because you are with me, I don't have to fear.
I really do have everything that I need.

If you weren't able to read the above confidently, try it again.

Resting with God in the Message

If you wish, read the passage again to yourself one more time.

As you've read the passage several times, how have you experienced God? What was God like? Reflect on how God seemed to you, especially if you sensed God walking beside you through the valley.

Allow yourself time to soak in the "with-ness" of God beside you, walking with you as your companion. Let it sink all the way down to where you really live. Sit for a few moments and ponder what has transpired. You may wish to:

- Sit and just "be" with God.
- Appreciate or celebrate what occurred in your conversation with God.
- Worship God by singing a song related to Psalm 23 (or even dancing to it). If you brought a recording of a Psalm 23 song, play it now. Close your eyes and listen.
- Rest in the idea that God is in the dark places with you, guiding you through, never leaving your side.
- Sit outside in the dark tonight with an empty chair next to you.
- Rest in the idea that God delights in you and in taking care of you.

Close the interaction with this prayer:

May today there be peace within.
May I trust you, God, that you can work in me exactly
    where I am.
May I not forget the infinite possibilities born of faith.
May I use those gifts I have received and pass on the love
    that has been given to me.
May I be content knowing I am your child.
Let your presence settle into my bones and allow my soul
    the freedom to sing, dance, praise, and love.
                    —THÉRÈSE OF LISIEUX (PARAPHRASED)

Move into a time of enjoying the life and breath God gave you.
You might want to:

- Take a nap
- Take a walk, hike, swim, or do relaxing exercises
- Try "porch sitting," watching birds and trees, or sitting in a
  Jacuzzi
- Do a creative activity (using art materials, woodworking,
  needlework, beadwork), without trying to accomplish
  anything
- Do light, meditative reading (not a detective novel or
  something that engages you wholly)

Trusting That God Is with Me

God could have chosen so many ways to relate to humans: making us robots that could be pushed around, going off and letting us be, using us for amusement. But it is God's nature to *be with* us, so this meditation repeats the important phrase "thou art with me," or "you are close beside me," and adds to it the images of the shepherd carrying a rod and staff. If you've had trouble picturing this passage so far (urban and suburban folks may never have encountered a sheep in a pasture, much less a shepherd's rod and staff), the pictures in these verses might bring some concreteness to your visualizing.

Opening to God's Message

Settle in the same space as before unless that proved to be distracting. (If the previous session is still resonating with you, pause for a moment. Do you want to do it again? If so, this is what retreatants call "repetitions." You may need to go deeper or broader.)

Set an empty chair next to you.

If you were to invite God to sit there, what would you say?

Why do you or don't you want God to sit there?

How close do you want that chair to be?

Do you want to face the chair or have it beside you?

Do you think God wants to sit there with you?

- Only if I behave
- Only when I'm quiet and read Scripture
- Only when I think good thoughts
- Only if I ask
- Other _____

Overall, how do you feel about the idea that God is *with* you and wants to be *with* you? Circle the five words that most describe how you feel about the idea and cross out the five that least fit.

Scared	Satisfied	Bewildered	Elated
Troubled	Powerful	Trusting	Rejected
Incompetent	Complete	Insecure	Foggy
Confident	Uneasy	Peaceful	Safe

Immersed in God's Message

CONTEXT: The two ideas in this verse—that God is with us and that God carefully protects us and helps us—are meant to be proof that we can believe that the Lord really is our shepherd and we really do have everything we need.

To quiet yourself and focus before reading the passage, say this slowly:

> *In our meditation we ponder the chosen text on the strength of the promise that it has something utterly personal to say to us today and for our Christian life.*[1]

Read this Scripture passage aloud very slowly.

The Eternal shepherds me, I lack for nothing;
he makes me lie in meadows green,
he leads me to refreshing streams,
he revives life in me.

He guides me by true paths,
as he himself is true.
My road may run through a glen of gloom,
but I fear no harm, for thou art beside me;
thy club, thy staff—they give me courage. . . .

For you are close beside me.
Your rod and your staff
    protect and comfort me. (Psalm 23:1-4, Moffatt;
      verse 4, NLT)

Before reading the passage again, consider:

MEANING OF WORDS: The *rod* is primarily an instrument of protection. Moffatt called it a club. The skilled shepherd "uses the rod to drive off predators like coyotes, wolves, cougars or stray dogs. Often it is used to beat the brush, discouraging snakes and other creatures from disturbing the flock."[2]

The rod is also used for guidance in the sense of discipline, to push or startle a sheep who has wandered near poisonous weeds or some other danger.[3] How was the shepherd's rod a *comfort?* The rod is a much-needed "extension of the owner's right arm. It stood as a symbol of his strength, his power, his authority in any serious situation. . . . There was comfort and consolation in seeing the rod in the shepherd's skillful hands"[4] because that meant the sheep were being watched over.

MEANING OF WORDS: The *staff* is a long slender stick often with a crook or hook on one end, and it has been shaped and smoothed by its owner. It was used primarily to guide sheep where they needed to go: pulling a lamb to its mother, guiding sheep away from dangerous drop-offs. The shepherd also uses the staff to rescue sheep, to do such things as pull them out of ravines or free them from being entangled in thorns. *The Message* communicates this: "Your trusty shepherd's crook makes me feel secure."

WRONG IMPRESSIONS: Neither the rod nor the staff is used to beat the sheep. Some people feel that God is beating up on them through circumstances or certain scriptures. Psalm 23:4 has even been used to indicate that God uses a rod to "get after" people and reprimand them. The image here is not that. The shepherd is not punitive but watchful, providing everything we need.

THEME OF SCRIPTURE: The idea that God is with us is one of the pervasive themes of Scripture. God chooses to relate to us, not to scrutinize us but to *be with* us. Even when we make mistakes, God is still with us. For example, after the Israelites fell into idolatry and were taken captive, God brought them back, helping them to rebuild the temple and saying, "I am with you" and "Be strong . . . and work. For I am with you" (Haggai 1:13; 2:4).

God is ever relational and eager to interact with us. "This personal interaction is what we see people in the Bible experiencing: God surrounding humans with hidden protection, God coming alongside them in battle, God wanting to 'hold their hand,' and God initiating good things in people's lives, including correction (see 2 Kings 6:17; 2 Chronicles 20:17; Isaiah 42:6; Nehemiah 9)."[5]

PICTURING THE PASSAGE: You might see yourself in a dangerous situation yet unaware of the danger until you hear the shepherd's rod whistling through the air to attack the dog or snake that is about to pounce on you. Even when we are unaware of God, God is always aware and watching.

PICTURING THE PASSAGE: You might envision yourself stranded alone in a ravine and first *hearing* the shepherd's voice, then *seeing* the shepherd's face, and then *seeing* the staff move toward you to pull you out of the crevice you are stuck in. Feel that joy and excitement.

As you read the Scripture passage again aloud, consider what word, phrase, or image from verse 4 stands out to you. Be open to letting God speak to you. Expect to be surprised. Be open to dialoguing with God.

The Eternal shepherds me, I lack for nothing;
he makes me lie in meadows green,
he leads me to refreshing streams,
he revives life in me.

He guides me by true paths,
as he himself is true.
My road may run through a glen of gloom,

but I fear no harm, for thou art beside me;
thy club, thy staff—they give me courage. . . .

For you are close beside me.
Your rod and your staff
    protect and comfort me.

Write down the word, phrase, idea, or image that stands out to you.

What feelings did you get in these verses?

What thoughts or impressions come to you? What connections do you make? What questions or perhaps objections do you have? Does anything surprise you?

What might God be saying to you through what has stood out in this passage?

Responding to God's Message

Read the passage again to yourself and continue to consider how it leads you to dialogue with God.

> The Eternal shepherds me, I lack for nothing;
> he makes me lie in meadows green,
> he leads me to refreshing streams,
> he revives life in me.
>
> He guides me by true paths,
> as he himself is true.
> My road may run through a glen of gloom,
> but I fear no harm, for thou art beside me;
> thy club, thy staff—they give me courage. . . .
>
> For you are close beside me.
> Your rod and your staff
> protect and comfort me.

Write your prayer response in the space provided or say it aloud. Be open to having a dialogue with God, to being gently led by the Holy Spirit.

If you're not sure what to pray, here are some possibilities:

- Talk about how you respond to God wanting to *be with* us.
- Ask God to use the rod or staff to help you in some way.
- Tell God how much you do or don't have a sense of God providing everything you need.

- Begin with, "I'm so glad that you said . . ." or "I really needed to hear that you . . ."

After you're finished praying, try this experiment again.

"TRYING ON" THE PSALM: Read this paraphrase of verses 1-4 aloud in a confident voice. Don't worry if you don't mean every word it says or even most words. For now you're trying on the idea of living your life in the kingdom of God—of trusting God, no matter what. Even if it doesn't fit, try it on.

You really are my shepherd—all day long.
You really do give me everything I need—all day long.
You really do make me lie down in green pastures
and lead me beside still waters—all day long.
You really do restore my soul—all day long.
You really do guide me in the best kinds of paths because you
always do what's best for me—all day long.
You really are with me even when I walk through very dark
things—all day long.
Because you are with me, I don't have to fear.
I really do have everything that I need—all day long.
You really comfort me with your readiness to use your rod to
protect me and your staff to guide me—all day long.

If you weren't able to read the paraphrase confidently, try it again.

Resting with God in the Message

As you've read the passage several times, how have you experienced God? What was God like? Reflect on how God seemed to you. Did God seem to want to be with you? Was God glad to sit beside you or just doing you a favor and eager to get away? Talk to God about this.

Allow yourself time to soak in what has come to you—questions, new ideas, and clarifications about God or yourself. Let it sink all the way down to where you really live. Sit for a few moments and ponder what has transpired.

If you've taken a break and the empty chair from the opening of this chapter is not next to you now, set an empty chair beside you. Let that empty chair's position represent to you how God wants to be with you. Pull the chair as close or far away as you think is appropriate.

Sit in the feeling of what it feels like to have God next to you. If you wish, say aloud, "You are close beside me and . . ." Or if you wish:

- Sit and just "be" with God.
- Appreciate or celebrate what occurred in your conversation with God.
- Worship God by singing a song related to Psalm 23 (or even dancing to it). If you brought a recording of a Psalm 23 song, play it now. Close your eyes and listen.
- Rest in the idea that God delights in you and in taking care of you.

Close the interaction with this prayer:

May today there be peace within.
May I trust you, God, that you can work in me exactly
    where I am.
May I not forget the infinite possibilities born of faith.
May I use those gifts I have received and pass on the love
    that has been given to me.
May I be content knowing I am your child.
Let your presence settle into my bones and allow my soul
    the freedom to sing, dance, praise, and love.
        —THÉRÈSE OF LISIEUX (PARAPHRASED)

Move into a time of enjoying the life and breath God gave you.
You might want to take a walk or hike and find a long slender stick and
bring it back with you. You may wish to smooth it down by rubbing
leaves or cloth on it. Try to get it to fit with your size so that you could
easily use it to protect and guide a creature beside you. If you wish,
color it. Or:

- Take a nap
- Swim or do relaxing exercises
- Try "porch sitting," watching birds and trees, or sitting in a
  Jacuzzi
- Do a creative activity (using art materials, woodworking,
  needlework, beadwork), without trying to accomplish
  anything
- Do light, meditative reading (not a detective novel or
  something that engages you wholly)

Trusting God with Those Who Oppose Me

f we're going to trust that the Lord really is our shepherd and that we really do have everything we need today, we're going to interact with our enemies very differently. Although we think of enemies as people who have harmed us terribly, in reality an enemy is anyone we find difficult to love or just anyone we find difficult today. In this chapter's Scripture passage, a scene occurs in which the psalmist sits across the table from an enemy. Who would you prefer not to sit across the table from? At a meal with your extended family or your church, who would you prefer not to sit next to? This passage talks about how we can sit there in perfect peace. It creates a rich scene that you may enter into and perhaps experience God in some new ways.

Opening to God's Message

Even if you don't like poetry, please don't skip this next section. A simple little story in the form of a poem will help you understand the passage better. You'll enjoy it. The poem was written by the sixteenth-century much-admired poet and Anglican priest George Herbert and it creates an interesting scene between a host and a guest. The person speaking is the guest at a meal, but this guest is rather flabbergasted to be the guest when he sees who the host is. The host is identified only as "Love" (lines 1, 8, 11, 15, 17) and "quick-ey'd Love" (line 3).

In the first stanza, Love asks the poet if he needs anything (following a similar theme to Psalm 23:1). Stanza 2 is a conversation between Love and the poet. The poet speaks lines 7, 9, and 10. Love speaks lines 8 and 12, and smiles in line 11. Stanza 3 continues the conversation. Love speaks in lines 15 and 17. The poet speaks the other lines, except the last, in which the poet does the action (which prepares us to experience Psalm 23:5).

Read the entire poem aloud. If you wish, change voices with the speakers. Imagine the scene. Try to put yourself in the poet's place. How do you feel at the end of stanza 1? At the end of stanza 2? At the end of stanza 3?

Love

Stanza 1

1   Love bade me welcome, yet my soul drew back,
2   Guilty of dust and sin.
3   But quick-ey'd Love, observing me grow slack
4   From my first entrance in,
5   Drew nearer to me, sweetly questioning
6   If I lack'd anything.

Stanza 2

7   "A guest," I answer'd, "worthy to be here";
8   Love said, "You shall be he."
9   "I, the unkind, the ungrateful? ah my dear,
10 I cannot look on thee."
11 Love took my hand and smiling did reply,
12 "Who made the eyes but I?"

Stanza 3

13   "Truth, Lord, but I have marr'd them; let my
       shame

14   Go where it doth deserve."

15   "And know you not," says Love, "who bore the
       blame?"

16   "My dear, then I will serve."

17   "You must sit down," says Love,
       "and taste my meat."

18   So I did sit and eat.

—GEORGE HERBERT

Immersed in God's Message

CONTEXT: In this verse's image, God is still providing everything we need, including food and drink. The startling thing God provides here is not only protection from an enemy but also two other important things: (1) inner peace so we can actually eat in the company of our enemy; (2) the enemy's respect for us as the enemy looks on while we are honored and rejoiced in by God. God provides not only food and shelter but also meaning in life and a sense of worth.

To quiet yourself and focus before reading the passage, say this slowly:

> In our meditation we ponder the chosen text on the strength of the promise that it has something utterly personal to say to us today and for our Christian life.[1]

Read this passage aloud very slowly.

You prepare a table before me
    in the presence of my enemies;
you anoint my head with oil;
        my cup overflows. . . .

You prepare a banquet for me, where all my enemies can see
me; you welcome me as an honored guest and fill my cup to
the brim. . . .

Thou art my host, spreading a feast for me,
while my foes have to look on!
Thou hast poured oil upon my head,
my cup is brimming over. . . .

You serve me a six-course dinner
    right in front of my enemies.
You revive my drooping head;
        my cup brims with blessing. . . .

Thou preparest a table before me in the presence of mine
enemies: thou anointest my head with oil; my cup runneth
over. . . .

You prepare a feast for me
    in the presence of my enemies.
You welcome me as a guest,
        anointing my head with oil.
            My cup overflows with blessings. (Psalm 23:5, NRSV, GNT,
Moffatt, MSG, KJV, NLT)

Before reading the verses again, consider:

MEANING OF ACTIONS: Anointing with oil is symbolic for rejoicing and is used on festive occasions. It often indicates that a person is being set aside for a special task, such as when Samuel anointed both Saul and David to be king of Israel (see 1 Samuel 10:1; 16:13).

MEANING OF WORDS: *my cup overflows* The generous host provides much more drink than is needed. The cup seems bottomless—you take a drink and there's still enough (more than enough). A full cup to drink is a great help when dealing with an enemy. The throat gets dry from stress. In case we choke up, there's a full cup of liquid to help out.

PICTURING THE PASSAGE: Picture yourself at a table. Opposite you is seated someone who is an enemy of some kind: someone who has thwarted you, who annoys you, who has made your life difficult, who looks down on you.

As you sit there, God comes up behind you and begins gently pouring oil on your head to anoint you. This signals to your enemy that you are someone special whom God has anointed and that you are protected. You might imagine God's palms resting on your shoulders, maybe God even leaning over you in endearment. Can you feel God standing behind you this way? You are not only special to God but also useful—that's why you're being anointed for a task.

Also, God leans over from behind you and continually fills your cup. There's hardly any cup brim showing because it seems to overflow with the liquid you love to drink with your meal. You have found your still waters—you will never be thirsty again. And your enemy sees how well God provides for you; you have everything you need, and he or she will not dare attack you. As you sit across from your difficult person and you see your cup overflowing, you might be led to offer that person some of your drink because he or she seems thirsty.

As you read the verses either aloud or to yourself, consider what word, phrase, or image resonates with you.

You prepare a table before me
    in the presence of my enemies;
you anoint my head with oil;
    my cup overflows. . . .

You prepare a banquet for me, where all my enemies can see me; you welcome me as an honored guest and fill my cup to the brim. . . .

Thou art my host, spreading a feast for me,
while my foes have to look on!
Thou hast poured oil upon my head,
my cup is brimming over. . . .

You serve me a six-course dinner
    right in front of my enemies.
You revive my drooping head;
    my cup brims with blessing. . . .

Thou preparest a table before me in the presence of mine enemies: thou anointest my head with oil; my cup runneth over. . . .

You prepare a feast for me
    in the presence of my enemies.
You welcome me as a guest,
    anointing my head with oil.
    My cup overflows with blessings.

Write down the word, phrase, or idea that stands out to you.

What feelings do you get in these verses?

What thoughts or impressions come to you? What connections do you make? What questions or perhaps objections do you have? Does anything surprise you?

What might God be saying to you through what has stood out in this passage?

Responding to God's Message

Read again verse 5 from the Bible translation that most resonated with you and consider how it leads you to dialogue with God.

> You prepare a table before me
>   in the presence of my enemies;
> you anoint my head with oil;
>   my cup overflows. . . .

> You prepare a banquet for me, where all my enemies can see me; you welcome me as an honored guest and fill my cup to the brim. . . .

> Thou art my host, spreading a feast for me,
> while my foes have to look on!
> Thou hast poured oil upon my head,
> my cup is brimming over. . . .

> You serve me a six-course dinner
>   right in front of my enemies.
> You revive my drooping head;
>   my cup brims with blessing. . . .

> Thou preparest a table before me in the presence of mine enemies: thou anointest my head with oil; my cup runneth over. . . .

> You prepare a feast for me
>   in the presence of my enemies.
> You welcome me as a guest,
>   anointing my head with oil.
>   My cup overflows with blessings.

Write your prayer response in the space provided or say it aloud. Be open to having a dialogue with God, to being gently led by the Holy Spirit. If you're not sure how to begin, here are some possibilities:

- Begin by writing, "While I was seated at the table . . ."
- Describe feeling as though you don't deserve to be treated so well (as the guest in Herbert's poem felt). Are you willing to stay at the table and see what happens?

After you're finished praying, try this experiment again.

"TRYING ON" THE PSALM: Read this paraphrase of verses 1-5 aloud in a confident a voice. Don't worry if you don't mean every word it says. For now, you're trying on the idea of living your life in the kingdom of God—of trusting God, no matter what.

You really are my shepherd—no matter what.
You really do give me everything I need—no matter what.
You really do make me lie down in green pastures
and lead me beside still waters—no matter what.
You really do restore my soul—no matter what.
You really do guide me in the best kinds of paths because you
always do what's best for me—no matter what.
You really are with me even when I walk through very dark

things—no matter what.

Because you are with me, I don't have to fear—no matter what.

I really do have everything that I need—no matter what.

You really comfort me with your readiness to use your rod to protect me and your staff to guide me—no matter what.

You really do care for me and how lost I feel—no matter what: you set up a table for my enemy and me and honor me (by anointing me)—right there in front of that person! You provide me with more than enough to refresh myself—no matter what.

If you weren't able to read the paraphrase confidently, try it again.

Resting with God in the Message

As you've read the passage several times, how have you experienced God? What was God like? Reflect on how God seemed to you. Talk to God about this.

Now sit at a table and soak in the idea of being able to be there unafraid and quite comfortable even if an enemy is across from you. Then, if you wish, read the version that resonates best with you one more time. Allow yourself time to soak in what you've experienced in this passage.

You prepare a table before me
    in the presence of my enemies;
you anoint my head with oil;
    my cup overflows. . . .

You prepare a banquet for me, where all my enemies can see me; you welcome me as an honored guest and fill my cup to the brim. . . .

Thou art my host, spreading a feast for me,
while my foes have to look on!
Thou hast poured oil upon my head,
my cup is brimming over. . . .

You serve me a six-course dinner
    right in front of my enemies.
You revive my drooping head;
        my cup brims with blessing. . . .

Thou preparest a table before me in the presence of mine enemies: thou anointest my head with oil; my cup runneth over. . . .

You prepare a feast for me
    in the presence of my enemies.
You welcome me as a guest,
        anointing my head with oil.
        My cup overflows with blessings.

You may wish to:

- Sit and just "be" with God.
- Appreciate or celebrate what occurred in your conversation with God.
- Worship God by singing a song related to Psalm 23 (or even dancing to it). If you brought a recording of a Psalm 23 song, play it now. Close your eyes and listen.

- Rest in the idea that God stands behind you, supporting you.
- Rest in the idea that God delights in you and in providing everything you need.

Close the interaction with this prayer:

May today there be peace within.
May I trust you, God, that you can work in me exactly
     where I am.
May I not forget the infinite possibilities born of faith.
May I use those gifts I have received and pass on the love
     that has been given to me.
May I be content knowing I am your child.
Let your presence settle into my bones and allow my soul
     the freedom to sing, dance, praise, and love.
                    —THÉRÈSE OF LISIEUX (PARAPHRASED)

Move into a time of enjoying the life and breath God gave you.
You might want to:

- Take a nap
- Take a walk, hike, swim, or do relaxing exercises
- Try "porch sitting," watching birds and trees, or sitting in a Jacuzzi
- Do a creative activity (using art materials, woodworking, needlework, beadwork), without trying to accomplish anything
- Do light, meditative reading (not a detective novel or something that engages you wholly)

A Life of Settled Trust in God

The psalmist talks about how to walk through scary situations with God as a companion. When we do so, we live unafraid and so we behave very differently. To ponder what that's like, ask yourself this question again: What would you do if you weren't afraid? In certain situations? In all of life? What would your life be like? Who would benefit?

The psalm now moves to a picture of what life looks like for the people who trust God for everything. Their settled way of being looks like this: goodness (that deep inner attractive goodness) and mercy well up from them in a quiet way so that you like being around them. They live in the kingdom of God, so they have steady interaction with the indwelling God in all of life.

Opening to God's Message

Settle in your usual place. If you find you're distracted by realizing this is your last session, soothe yourself by noting that this session is about the person you are becoming and will continue to be in your normal life that you're about to step back into. (If the previous session is still resonating with you, pause for a moment. Do you want to do it again? If so, this is what retreatants call "repetitions." You may need to go deeper or broader.)

Think about a person who lives in an atmosphere of goodness and mercy, whose life is clearly lived in the companionship of God. This can be someone you know, a fictional character, or someone you can imagine.

What word (or two or three) would you use to describe that person?

What color does his or her life bring to mind?

What texture (rocky, corduroy, marble) does his or her life bring to mind?

When in your life do you most need this sort of settled way of being?

Immersed in God's Message

CONTEXT: Verse 6 is a picture of what our life looks like when we trust that the Lord is our shepherd and we have everything we need as a matter of normal everyday practice.

TONE: As the psalm progresses, it takes a more personal tone, and the words *I* and *me* become more prominent.

> In some other contexts (as in the lament of Psalm 77), the repeated reference to self sounds like an unhealthy obsession. But here that is not the case. Here the "I" statements are filled with gratitude, yielding, trust, and thanksgiving. The "I" here knows that in every case, life is fully cared for and resolved by this thou who responds to and anticipates every need. Life with [God] is a life of well-being and satisfaction.[1]

To quiet yourself and focus before reading the passage, say this slowly:

> *In our meditation we ponder the chosen text on the strength of the promise that it has something utterly personal to say to us today and for our Christian life.*[2]

Read this Scripture passage aloud very slowly.

The LORD is my shepherd, I shall not be in want.
  He makes me lie down in green pastures,
he leads me beside quiet waters,
  he restores my soul.
He guides me in paths of righteousness
  for his name's sake.
Even though I walk
  through the valley of the shadow of death,
I will fear no evil,
  for you are with me;
your rod and your staff,
  they comfort me.

You prepare a table before me
    in the presence of my enemies.
You anoint my head with oil;
    my cup overflows.
Surely goodness and love will follow me
    all the days of my life,
and I will dwell in the house of the LORD
    forever. . . .

Your beauty and love chase after me
    every day of my life.
I'm back home in the house of GOD
    for the rest of my life. . . .

Surely your goodness and unfailing love will pursue me
    all the days of my life,
and I will live in the house of the Lord
    forever. . . .

Yes, and all through my life
Goodness and Kindness wait on me,
the Eternal's guest
within his household evermore. (Psalm 23:1-6, NIV; verse 6,
MSG, NLT, Moffatt)

Before reading the passage again, consider the following.

MEANING OF WORDS: *Goodness* is true in every sense of the word and is often translated "pleasant" or "delightful."[3]

MEANING OF WORDS: *Mercy* is often translated "love" or "steadfast love." This is the Hebrew word *hesed* or *chesedh,* an idea so immense that no single English word can be found to translate it accurately. *Hesed* encompasses the ideas of loving-kindness, mercy, unwavering loyalty, and truth. God abounds in *hesed,* which is described in various passages as far-reaching, overflowing, everlasting, astonishing, satisfying, enduring, saving, and drawing (see Psalms 33:5; 103:11,17; 17:7; 90:14; 136:1; 85:7; Jeremiah 31:3). As we trust God to provide everything we need, we live our life in the atmosphere of God's *hesed.*

IDEAS: Goodness and mercy *follow me.* When certain people leave a room, they leave an atmosphere or trail behind them of peace or turmoil, resolution or conflict, joy or frustration, love or animosity. People who trust that God is their shepherd leave a trail of goodness (deep inner goodness that's attractive) and mercy (helping others and forgiving mistakes). The room is an easier place to be in when they have been there. Compared to verse 5, the psalmist is now "no longer hunted down by his enemies, but he is literally pursued by the goodness of God. Furthermore, this is no temporary situation but it is going to be the characteristic of his whole life."[4]

MEANING OF WORDS: *dwell in the house of the Lord forever* People who trust God and God's provision live lives of ongoing, enduring, stable well-being. They have "continual communion with God"[5] and fellowship with God, dwelling in the love, joy, and peace of God. The settled attitude of their souls is one of trust.

GETTING INSIDE THE PASSAGE: You might picture yourself doing things that feel good and right and true and also give you great joy. What color would you assign to such a life?

You might guess what it feels like to live your life in an atmosphere of goodness and deep mercy. What color would you assign to having a settled attitude of trust in one's life?

You may guess what it feels like to live your life in the continual companionship (dwelling) of God. What color would you assign to having a settled attitude of trust in one's life?

What do these colors tell you about such a life?

As you read the Scripture passage, consider what word, phrase, or idea stands out to you or resonates with you, especially from verse 6.

The LORD is my shepherd, I shall not be in want.
> He makes me lie down in green pastures,
he leads me beside quiet waters,
> he restores my soul.
He guides me in paths of righteousness
> for his name's sake.
Even though I walk
> through the valley of the shadow of death,
I will fear no evil,
> for you are with me;
your rod and your staff,
> they comfort me.

You prepare a table before me
> in the presence of my enemies.
You anoint my head with oil;
> my cup overflows.
Surely goodness and love will follow me
> all the days of my life,

and I will dwell in the house of the LORD
        forever. . . .

Your beauty and love chase after me
        every day of my life.
I'm back home in the house of GOD
        for the rest of my life. . . .

Surely your goodness and unfailing love will pursue me
        all the days of my life,
and I will live in the house of the Lord
        forever. . . .

Yes, and all through my life
Goodness and Kindness wait on me,
the Eternal's guest
within his household evermore.

Write down the word, phrase, or idea that stands out to you.

What feelings did you get from these verses?

What thoughts or impressions come to you? What connections do you make? What questions or perhaps objections do you have? Does anything surprise you?

What might God be saying to you through what has stood out in this passage?

Responding to God's Message

Read again the translation of verse 6 that most resonated with you and consider how it leads you to dialogue with God.

> Surely goodness and love will follow me
>   all the days of my life,
> and I will dwell in the house of the LORD
>   forever. . . .

> Your beauty and love chase after me
>   every day of my life.
> I'm back home in the house of GOD
>   for the rest of my life. . . .

Surely your goodness and unfailing love will pursue me
    all the days of my life,
and I will live in the house of the Lord
    forever. . . .

Yes, and all through my life
Goodness and Kindness wait on me,
the Eternal's guest
within his household evermore.

Write your prayer response in the space provided or say it aloud. If you're not sure what to say, talk to God about the life of goodness, mercy, and constant communion described in this verse. Do you want it? What might it take to get it? Be open to having a dialogue with God, to being gently led by the Holy Spirit.

Now pray the entire psalm back to God by adding phrases as needed.[6] You don't have to pray every line, and you don't have to pray them in order. Here are some starter lines:

- "You, O God, are my shepherd. You . . ."
- "You provide everything I need (*when* or *how* or *because*) . . ."

- "You make me lie down in green pastures (*such as* or *when*) . . ."
- "You lead me beside still waters (*such as* or *when*) . . ."
- "You restore my soul (*every time* or *when*) . . .
- "You lead me in the best possible paths (*would you do this?*)."
- "You are with me when I walk through valleys (*such as* or *help me with this*) . . ."
- "I will fear no evil, O God, because thou art with me. (*I know this because* or *Help me to know this*) . . ."
- "Your protection and guidance keep me safe. (*I have seen this when* or *I need to see this when*) . . ."
- "Even when I am around such difficult people, you (*honor me by* or *you fill all my needs*) . . ."
- "I'm confident that your beautiful goodness and deep mercy (*will fill me* or *will surround me*) . . ."
- "I'm so glad that you are the companion of my soul forever."

Resting with God in the Message

As you've read the passage several times, how have you experienced God? What was God like? Reflect on how God seemed to you. Full of peace or turmoil, resolution or conflict, joy or frustration, love or animosity? Talk to God about this.

Allow yourself time to soak in the word, phrase, or idea from verse 6 that resonated with you — questions, new ideas and clarifications about God or yourself. Go over it. Soak in it. Let it sink all the way down to where you really live. Sit for a few moments and ponder what has transpired. You may wish to:

- Sit and just "be" with God.
- Appreciate or celebrate what occurred in your conversation with God.
- Worship God by singing a song related to Psalm 23 (or even dancing to it). If you brought a recording of a Psalm 23 song, play it now. Close your eyes and listen.
- Rest in the idea that God delights in you and in taking care of you.

Close the interaction with this prayer:

May today there be peace within.
May I trust you, God, that you can work in me exactly
    where I am.
May I not forget the infinite possibilities born of faith.
May I use those gifts I have received and pass on the love
    that has been given to me.
May I be content knowing I am your child.
Let your presence settle into my bones and allow my soul
    the freedom to sing, dance, praise, and love.
    —THÉRÈSE OF LISIEUX (PARAPHRASED)

Before leaving your retreat site, pause. Thank God for this extended time. As you near home, start picturing the people who may be there, what they need from you, and what your tasks will be. Thank God for these people and ask God to help you welcome them. Once you arrive, keep moving as slowly as possible.

As you make your way home, ponder also what worked well about your personal retreat (location, setting, timing) so that your next retreat will bring an even more natural tendency to rest in God. Don't forget to continue to reflect on the retreat. Some of your best insights may be yet to come.

Notes

Introduction: Why Retreat? Making Space for God

1. David Takle, *The Truth About Lies and the Lies About Truth* (Pasadena, CA: Shepherd's House, 2008), 174.
2. Takle, 174.
3. Lynne Baab, "A Day Off from God Stuff," *Leadership Journal*, Spring 2007, http://www.christianitytoday.com/le/2007 /002/18.34.html.

Meditation 1: Does God Really Provide Everything I Need?

1. This is a summary of the Sermon on the Mount.
2. Walter Brueggeman, *The Message of the Psalms: A Theological Commentary* (Minneapolis: Augsburg, 1984), 152, emphasis added.
3. Dietrich Bonhoeffer, *Life Together* (New York: Harper & Row, 1954), 82.
4. Phillip Keller, *A Shepherd Looks at Psalm 23*, large print edition (Grand Rapids, MI: Zondervan, 1970), 31.
5. Brueggeman, 155.

Meditation 2: Trusting God for Soul Restoration

1. Dietrich Bonhoeffer, *Life Together* (New York: Harper & Row, 1954), 82.

2. A. A. Anderson, *The New Century Bible Commentary, Psalms (1-72)* (Grand Rapids, MI: Eerdmans, 1972), 195.

3. Phillip Keller, *A Shepherd Looks at Psalm 23* (Grand Rapids, MI: Zondervan, 1976), 50–51.

4. Keller, 35.

5. Anderson, 195.

6. F. Delitzsch, *Commentary on the Old Testament in Ten Volumes*, vol. V Psalms (Grand Rapids, MI: Eerdmans, 1973), 330.

Meditation 3: Trusting God to Lead

1. Dietrich Bonhoeffer, *Life Together* (New York: Harper & Row, 1954), 82.

2. A. A. Anderson, *The New Century Bible Commentary, Psalms (1-72)* (Grand Rapids, MI: Eerdmans, 1972), 195.

3. Dallas Willard, *The Divine Conspiracy: Rediscovering Our Hidden Life in God* (San Francisco: HarperSanFrancisco, 1998), 145, describing *dikaiosune*, which is how the Hebrew word *tseh'-dek* (Psalm 23:3) is normally translated into Greek.

4. H. C. Leupold, *Exposition of the Psalms* (Grand Rapids, MI: Baker, 1972), 212.

Meditation 4: Trusting God in the Deep Valleys

1. N. T. Wright, *Following Jesus* (Grand Rapids, MI: Eerdmans, 1994), 66.

2. Walter Brueggeman, *The Message of the Psalms: A Theological Commentary* (Minneapolis: Augsburg, 1984), 154.

3. Dietrich Bonhoeffer, *Life Together* (New York: Harper & Row, 1954), 82.

4. H. C. Leupold, *Exposition of the Psalms* (Grand Rapids, MI: Baker, 1969), 212.

5. Brueggeman, 155–156.

Meditation 5: Trusting That God Is with Me

1. Dietrich Bonhoeffer, *Life Together* (New York: Harper & Row, 1954), 82.
2. Phillip Keller, *A Shepherd Looks at Psalm 23*, large print edition (Grand Rapids, MI: Zondervan, 1970), 97.
3. Keller, 95.
4. Keller, 93–94.
5. Jan Johnson, *Invitation to the Jesus Life: Experiments in Christlikeness* (Colorado Springs, CO: NavPress, 2008), 17. See also 29–41.

Meditation 6: Trusting God with Those Who Oppose Me

1. Dietrich Bonhoeffer, *Life Together* (New York: Harper & Row, 1954), 82.

Meditation 7: A Life of Settled Trust in God

1. Walter Brueggeman, *The Message of the Psalms: A Theological Commentary* (Minneapolis: Augsburg, 1984), 156.
2. Dietrich Bonhoeffer, *Life Together* (New York: Harper & Row, 1954), 82.
3. W. E. Vine, Merrill F. Unger, William White Jr., *Vine's Expository Dictionary of Biblical Words* (Nashville: Thomas Nelson, 1985), 99.
4. A. A. Anderson, *The New Century Bible Commentary, Psalms (1-72)* (Grand Rapids, MI: Eerdmans, 1972), 199.
5. Anderson, 199.
6. This process is described by C. S. Lewis as "festooning." See C. S. Lewis, *Letters to Malcolm* (New York: Harcourt Brace and Company, 1964), 24.

About the Author

J an Johnson is the author of nineteen books, including *Savoring God's Word* and *When the Soul Listens,* and more than a thousand magazine articles and Bible studies. Also a speaker, teacher, and spiritual director, she lives with her husband in Simi Valley, California (www.janjohnson.org). She holds a DMin in Ignatian spirituality and spiritual direction and writes primarily about spiritual formation topics.

Learn from Jan Johnson how to grow in Christ.

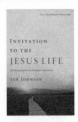

Invitation to the Jesus Life
Jan Johnson

978-1-60006-146-2

Would you like to be drenched with love, focused on others, and filled with courage? Jan Johnson offers a closer look at seventeen underrated qualities of Jesus to help you become more like Jesus. Spiritual practices, as well as questions and group-study suggestions, are included at the end of each chapter.

Learning to Hear God
Jan Johnson

978-1-60006-660-3

God desires a relationship with us, and relationships involve communication. This retreat guide encourages readers to rest quietly in God's arms and listen for God's words of love. Ideal for one- or three-day personal or group retreats. Includes seven self-contained sessions.

Living in the Companionship of God
Jan Johnson

978-1-60006-659-7

Get away from it all with God. This unique retreat guide can help direct your thoughts to the underlying needs of your soul. Ideal for one- or three-day personal or group retreats. Includes seven self-contained sessions.

To order copies, call NavPress at 1-800-366-7788 or log on to www.navpress.com.